JFK

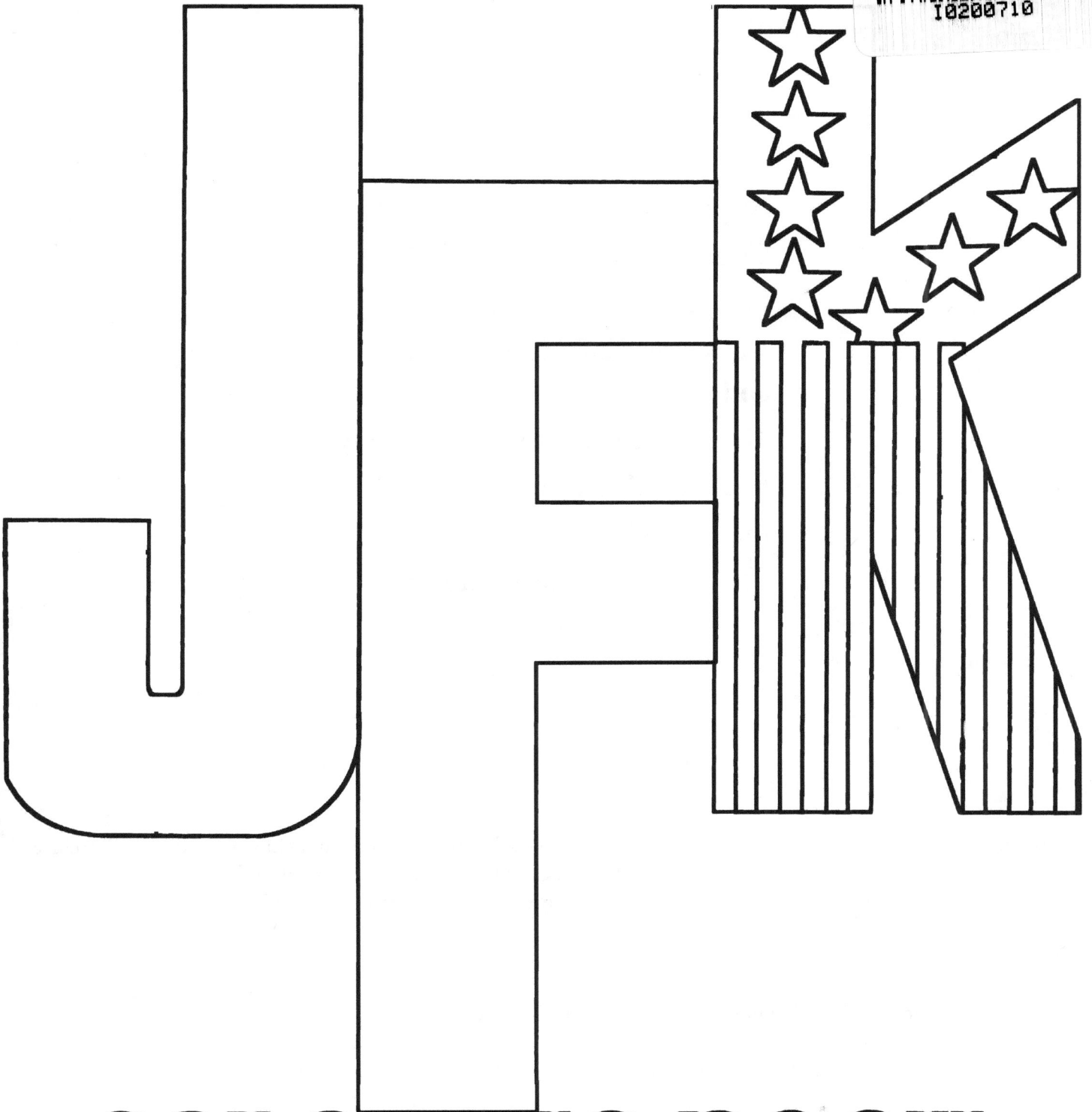

COLORING BOOK

ABOUT COMICS
Camarillo, California

Inspiration: R. Nixon

Conception: Alexander A. Roman

Drawings: Mort Drucker

Copy: Paul Laikin

and

(Man, like if the Prez doesn't dig
this bit, I don't want to be in
this alone.)

Jackie Kannon

About Comics would like to thank J.J. Gertler and the fine staff of the JFK Presidential Library Audiovisual Archives (including Maryrose Grossman, Kora Welsh, and David Castillo) for their help in identifying several of the caricatures. None of these people have vetted the text; any errors are not their responsibility.

JFK Coloring Book originally published by Kanrom, Inc., 1962.

Political Wind-Ups originally published by Kanrom, Inc., 1962.

Annotations created for this edition by About Comics.
Copyright 2014 About Comics.

ISBN: 978-1936404-48-3

Published September, 2014. November 2016 file edition.

For bulk orders, custom covers, or other inquiries, contact *questions@aboutcomics.com*

This is my Daddy.
He has a good job.
He works for the Government.
Color him red, white and blue.
My daddy is very important.
He has a lot of people working for him.
They would do anything for my daddy.
Color their noses burnt umber.

This is my Mommy.
She is very beautiful.
She is the most beautiful Mommy ever.
Color her beautiful.
See her pretty clothes?
They are very expensive.
They cost my daddy a lot of money.
Is that why he can't afford an overcoat?

4

See the pretty White House?
It is my pretty White House.
I live here.
Color it pretty white.
Better hurry up and color it.
Mommy is doing a lot of redecorating.
If you wait too long
You may have to color it Chartreuse.

See the funny chair?
It is daddy's funny chair.
It is a Rocking chair.
Daddy sits on it and rocks.
Rock, Rock, Rock.
My daddy loves his rocking chair.
My daddy is always sitting on it.
Daddy doesn't like to be off his rocker.

This is my Uncle.
See how young he is?
Color him green.
When he grows up he will get Daddy's job.
People say that he gives daddy orders.
I don't think daddy takes orders from him.
My daddy doesn't take orders from anybody.
Just Mommy.

See the nice man?
He is my other uncle.
Doesn't he look like Daddy?
Color him the same.
He is next in line for Daddy's job.
Now he is learning the business.
He will start at the bottom.
He will be in Congress.

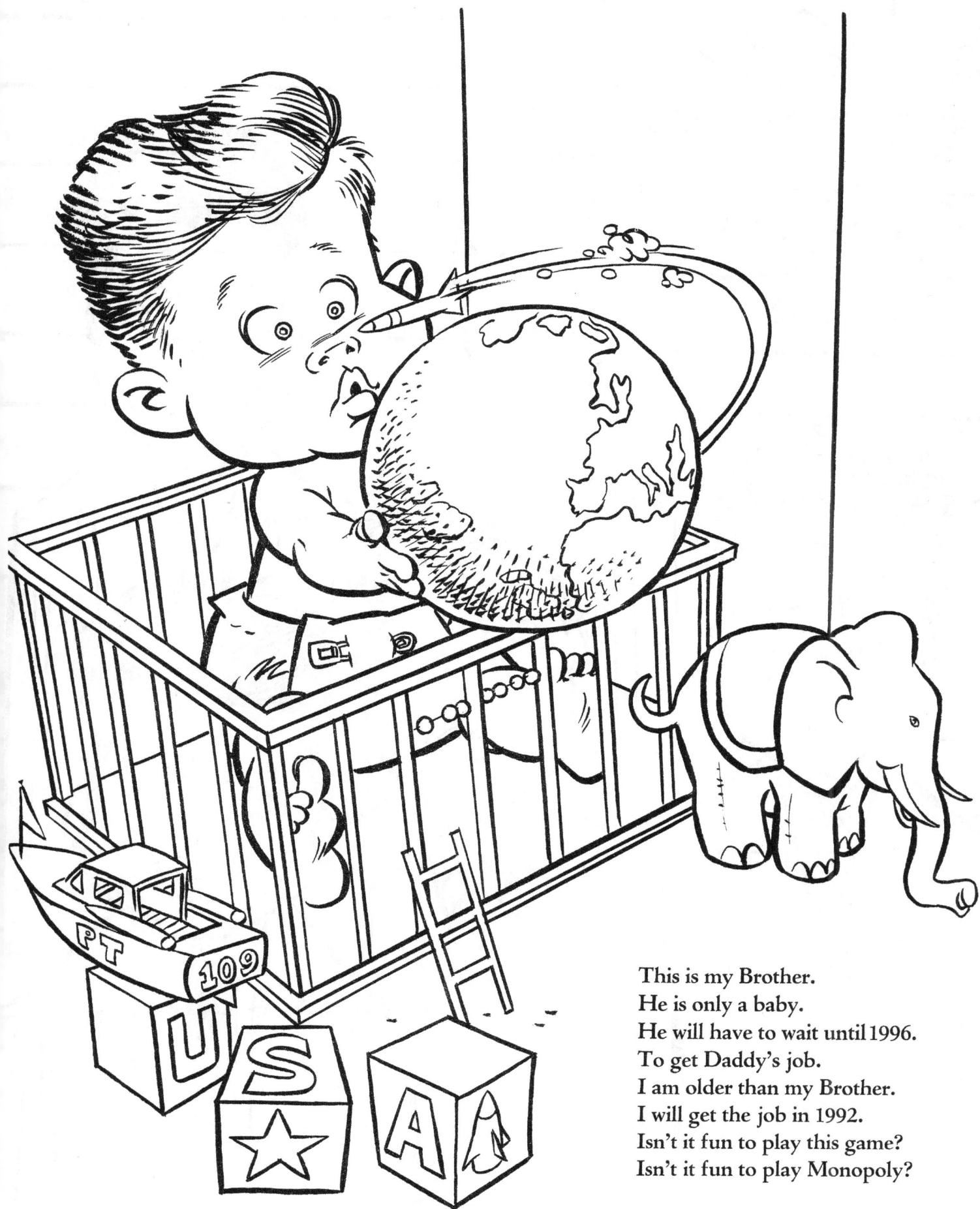

This is my Brother.
He is only a baby.
He will have to wait until 1996.
To get Daddy's job.
I am older than my Brother.
I will get the job in 1992.
Isn't it fun to play this game?
Isn't it fun to play Monopoly?

What is the Supreme Court?
Daddy says it will look like this one day.
Wouldn't that be fun?
You would never get mixed up.
There are ten men here.
Count them----Ten.
Daddy wants more people working.
Daddy loves everybody.

See the pretty lady?
She is my Aunt.
She is mommy's sister.
She says she's a Princess.
Where is her crown?
Where is her magic wand?
Is she really a Princess?
Do you think it's only a Fairy Tale?

See the handsome man?
He is my uncle too.
He is in show business.
He can sing and he can dance.
My aunt must have liked his song and dance.
But he will never get Daddy's job.
He belongs to another clan.
They have their own government.

This is Mommy's luggage.
See all the travel stickers?
Mommy is always traveling.
Daddy sends her on good will tours.
Some people say she is prettier than daddy.
My mommy is very popular.
She changes clothes four times a day.
The places she visits must be very dirty.

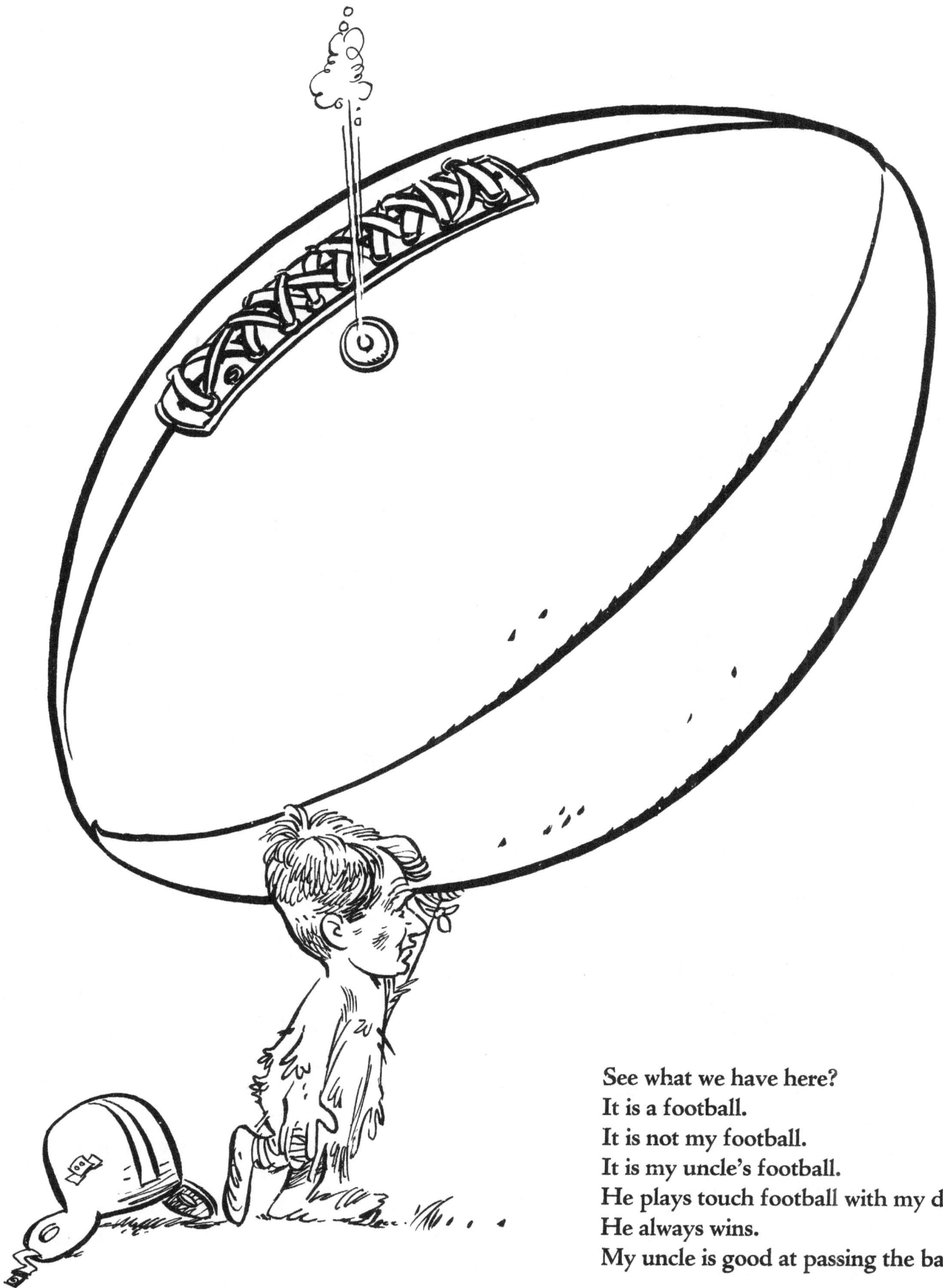

See what we have here?
It is a football.
It is not my football.
It is my uncle's football.
He plays touch football with my daddy.
He always wins.
My uncle is good at passing the ball.

Say hello to the fat jolly man.
Hello fat jolly man.
How are you today?
Will you give me another lollipop?
I didn't eat the last one you gave me.
Daddy told me not to.
Why didn't daddy want me to eat it?
Why did he make my doggie taste it first?

Look at all these people.
They are friends of the family.
They are always at our house.
They are very important.
Color them important.
I know almost everybody here.
Just that skinny one in the middle.
I wonder who he is?

See the cap and gown?
It is daddy's cap and gown.
Daddy went to Harvard.
Rah, Rah, Rah.
My daddy is very smart.
He used to work hard for his Professors.
Now his Professors work hard for him.
I told you my Daddy was smart!

See the nice man?
Say goodbye to him.
Goodbye nice man!
He is going away.
He is going on a nice long trip.
He will be away for a long time.
He will be the first man on the moon.
My family is sending him.

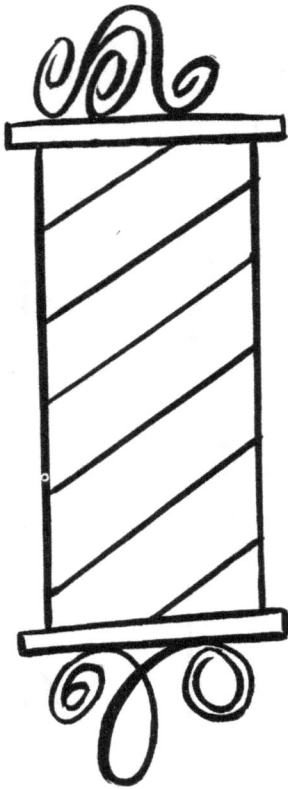

This is daddy's barber.
He is a man.
He is very poor.
He can't even make a living.
All year 'round.
Daddy never takes a haircut.

See the nice boat?
It is a yacht.
A yacht is a rich man's boat.
My daddy has two yachts.
My daddy goes on fishing trips.
My daddy always catches something.
My daddy has a good line.

See the man in the big hat?
He is daddy's helper.
He is very rich.
He comes from Texas.
He has a lot of oil wells.
He owns a big ranch.
He raises cattle.
He raises horses.
He raises lady birds.

This is Daddy's secretary.
He has a good job.
He tells people what daddy said.
He makes a lot of money.
Do you think that is fair?
I don't think that it is fair.
I tell people what Daddy said.
I get a licking.

This is the end.
It is the end of this book.
It is also the end of me.
Daddy has just seen this book.
Daddy says I talk too much.
Daddy says I tell too many secrets.
Daddy says I am too candid.
Daddy says I will never be a Politician.

Who's Who and What's What

Page 3: The large figure is JFK himself, President John Fitzgerald Kennedy.

The smaller figures are people JFK chose to represent the nation on the international scene. From left to right:

famed broadcaster Edward R. Murrow, who under Kennedy was the head of the United States Information Agency (the parent of Voice Of America). A committed chain-smoker, those cigarettes he's holding would be the death of him. he lived barely past his 57th birthday, with one lung removed due to lung cancer.

Adlai Stevenson II, JFK's ambassador to the United Nations.

Dean Rusk, JFK's Secretary of State, who would serve in that position until the end of the Johnson administration.

Page 4: Jaqueline Kennedy, first lady and fashion icon

Page 5: The golf ball in front of the White House would be a remnant of JFK's predecessor, Dwight David "Ike" Eisenhower, an addicted golfer.

Page 6: JFK took to rocking chairs in the 1950s at a doctor's suggestion; he so liked them that he made sure they were in all his residences and distributed them as gifts.

The donkey is the symbol of the Democratic Party, JFK's party.

Page 7: JFK's younger brother Bobby Kennedy served as Attorney General, where he took on organized crime, with vastly increased use of wiretaps and, as a result, vastly increased convictions.

Page 8: JFK's youngest brother Edward "Teddy" Kennedy took over JFK's former Senate seat via a special election in 1962. The book he's holding, Son of Profiles in Courage, is a reference to JFK's own book, Profiles in Courage. Teddy did eventually run for president in 1980, but lost the nomination to the incumbent president Jimmy Carter, who then lost the election to Ronald Reagan.

Page 9: John F. Kennedy, Jr., commonly known as John-John, never did run for office, although he kept the option open and was considered a front runner for the 2000 Senatorial election in New York… an election he did not live to see, dying in a plane crash in 1999. Hilary Clinton ran in and won that election; when she ceded the seat in order to take the roll of Secretary of State in the Obama administration, John-John's older sister Caroline (who narrates this book) expressed an interest in taking the seat, but chose to withdraw from consideration after about a month.

The boat marked PT 109 is a reference to the Patrol Torpedo boat that JFK commanded during World War II.

Pages 10-11: despite the gag here, JFK nominated no actual Kennedys to the Supreme Court, and didn't put forth any black candidates either. The two nominations he made, Byron White and Arthur Goldberg, were both male, but that is not particularly noteworthy as no females had previously been nominated, nor would any be until 1981. Both of JFK's nominations were confirmed.

Page 12: Jackie Kennedy's sister, Lee Radziwill, was indeed a princess, having married Poland's Prince Stanislaw Albrecht Radziwill in 1959. As Poland was under Soviet rule at the time, this was not a position of actual power.

Page 13: Actor Peter Lawford, a member of Hollywood's legendary Rat Pack (also known as "the Clan") married JFK's sister Patricia in 1954; they divorced in 1966.

Page 14: During her time as first lady, Jackie traveled to France, India, and Pakistan.

Page 15: The Kennedy family's tradition of touch football games on the lawn of their compound in Hyannis Port, Massachusetts, as recorded in home movies, captured the public's imagination.

Page 16: This is Soviet Premier Nikita Krushchev. The smaller figure in his pocket is longtime Cuban leader Fidel Castro.

Page 17: From left to right:
Lyndon Baines Johnson (LBJ) was JFK's vice president and successor.
Harry S. Truman served as President from 1945-1953
Frank Sinatra, the skinny one in the middle, was a hugely popular singer. As our narrator Caroline was only 4 years old at the time this was created, it's no surprise that she doesn't recognize him, but almost every adult in America would have.
Eleanor Roosevelt, as the wife of Franklin D. Roosevelt, was the First Lady of the US for twelve years (1933-1945) and a political force in her own right. She died a few months after this coloring book was first published.
Adlai Stevenson II, the grandson of Grover Cleveland's vice president Adlai Stevenson I, ran for the presidency himself on three occasions. In 1952 and 1956, he won the Democratic nomination but lost in the general election. In 1960, he lost the primary to JFK, who of course went on to win the election , and then chose Stevenson as his ambassador to the United Nations.

Page 18: JFK attended Harvard from 1936 to 1940, graduating cum laude.

Page 19: JFK was the man who set our manned space program going - but the individual seen here is no astronaut. Jimmy Hoffa, leader of the powerful International Brother of Teamsters (representing most notably long-haul truckers), was a target of investigation by Bobby Kennedy. The Transport Workers Union (TWU) would at times find themselves at odds with the Teamsters. As for whether there is any truth to this gag: Jimmy Hoffa hasn't been seen since 1975… but we haven't sent a man to check the moon since 1972, so maybe he is up there!

Page 20: JFK's hair, while generally neatly coiffed, was fuller than most men chose in those days. This goes hand-in-hand, so to speak, with his tendency not to wear a hat.

Page 21: JFK had two yachts as president; the 92-foot luxury yacht Honey Fitz was really Jackie's project, while the 62-foot Manitou was more of a yacht for a long time sail fan like JFK, as YachtPals.com describes it.

Page 22: Texan Lyndon Baines Johnson (LBJ) was JFK's vice president and successor. His wife, Claudia Alta Taylor Johnson, was commonly known as "Lady Bird".

Page 23: Pierre Salinger had been a key man in JFK's presidential campaign before becoming his press secretary. He also served as LBJ's press secretary, had a five month career in the Senate, worked extensively for ABC News, and appeared in one episode of the 1960s Batman series, playing "Lucky Pierre".

Page 24: Caroline Kennedy has not held political office yet.

POLITICAL WIND-UPS

Inspiration: JFK Coloring Book

Conception: Alexander A. Roman

Drawings: Mort Drucker

Added Copy: Rochelle Davis

and

Man, like I said before,

thank God it's a free country.

Jackie Kannon

JFK DOLL:

Wind it up and with lots of vigah it makes a judgment on Asier, Africer and Cuber.

BOBBY KENNEDY DOLL:

Wind it up and little Brother is watching you.

TEDDY KENNEDY DOLL:

Wind it up and it's Trick or Troika.

HARRY TRUMAN DOLL:

Wind it up and x # (! ? x $ X % /) ! .

BARRY GOLDWATER DOLL:

Wind it up and it moves forward into the nineteenth century.

RICHARD NIXON DOLL:

Wind it up and it cuts its own throat.

Wind it up and it hooks and slices for eight years.

NELSON ROCKEFELLER DOLL:

Wind it up and it runs like sixty...million.

MAYOR WAGNER DOLL:

Wind it up and it still does nothing.

JACKIE KENNEDY DOLL:

Wind it up and C'est Une Poupée.

JUSTICE BLACK DOLL:

Wind it up and you haven't got a prayer.

JIMMY HOFFA DOLL:

Wind it up and it gives you labor pains.

ESTES KEFAUVER DOLL:

Wind it up and it talks and talks and talks and talks and talks and talks.

WAYNE MORSE DOLL:

Wind it up and it goes from party to party.

GEORGE ROMNEY DOLL:

Wind it up and it stops driving like a Rambler and starts running like a Lincoln.

ORVAL FAUBUS DOLL:

Wind it up and it's in a class by itself.

DEAN RUSK DOLL:

Wind it up and it takes off without a plane.

ARTHUR SCHLESINGER DOLL:

Wind it up and *it writes courageous speeches on how to surrender.*

NEWTON MINOW DOLL:

Wind it up and it secretly watches gangster shows at home.

WESTBROOK PEGLER DOLL:

Wind it up and the verdict is unanimous.

MARTIN LUTHER KING DOLL:

Wind it up and it sits in back of the jail.

WALTER REUTHER DOLL:

Wind it up and you have two strikes against you.

EARL WARREN DOLL:

Wind it up and it's warming up on the bench.

WALTER WINCHELL DOLL:

Wind it up and it attacks the JFK Doll.

NASSER DOLL:

Wind it up and it's the Shriek of Araby.

JAWAHARLAL NEHRU DOLL:

Wind it in neutral & it Goa's into reverse.

BEN GURION DOLL:

Wind it up and goes till Friday night.

PRINCESS GRACE DOLL:

Wind it up and it plays the Palace.

FIDEL CASTRO DOLL:

Wind it up and it shaves and turns out to be Batista.

MAO TSE TUNG DOLL:

Wind it up and you don't have a Chinaman's chance.

SUKARNO DOLL:

Wind it up and it becomes a neutral communist.

FAROUK DOLL:

Wind it and wind it and it still sits on its big fat Cannes.

MOISE TSHOMBE DOLL:

Wind it up and it has you for dinner.

KRISHNA MENON DOLL:

Wind it up and it's the world's worst fakir.

GENERALISSIMO FRANCO DOLL:

Wind it up and it lives on a diet of lemonade, orangeade and foreignade.

SHAH OF IRAN DOLL:

Wind it up and it turns a slim princess into a Persian melon.

HAROLD MACMILLAN DOLL:

Wind it up and it restocks the cabinet.

CHARLES DE GAULLE DOLL:

Wind it up and it grows so tall — it can't see eye-to-eye with anybody.

CHIANG KAI-SHEK DOLL:

Wind it up and it keeps repeating "No man is an island."

KONRAD ADENAUER DOLL:

Wind it up and it puts Deutschland uber Allies.

KHRUSHCHEV DOLL:

We had better wind it up before it winds us up.

Who were these people, and what happened to them?

JFK: John Fitzgerald Kennedy, previously a US Senator from Massachusetts and with a strong Boston accent to match, served as president of the United States from January 20, 1961 until his assassination on November 22, 1963.

Bobby Kennedy: JFK's brother served as the Attorney General in JFK's administration and after his death. In 1964, he was elected Senator from New York, a position he held when he was assassinated in 1968 during his campaign for president.

Teddy Kennedy: The youngest Kennedy brother took over JFK's former Senate seat via a special election in 1962. He held the seat until his death from natural causes in 2009.

Harry Truman: Having risen to the presidency upon the death of Franklin Roosevelt in 1945, he served in the office 1953. He died in 1972 from complications from pneumonia.

Barry Goldwater: A Senator from Arizona at the time this book was created, "Mr. Conservative" Goldwater would go on to run for the presidency in 1964, gaining the Republican Party's nomination but losing in the final race to Lyndon Johnson. He returned to the Senate, leaving in 1987 and dying from a stroke in 1998.

Richard Nixon: Having served as Vice President for eight years under President Dwight Eisenhower, Nixon was the Republican candidate who lost to JFK in the 1960 presidential election. Immediately following the loss, he announced to the press that they "won't have Nixon to kick around any more," but he would later resurface politically, winning the presidential elections of 1968 and 1972 before resigning in disgrace in 1974. Nixon died in 1994.

Dwight Eisenhower: The president who preceded JFK was a passionate golfer. He died in 1969.

Nelson Rockefeller: An heir to the vast Rockefeller fortune, Nelson served as governor of New York from 1959 to 1973, and took the post of Vice President in 1974 when Gerald Ford ascended to the presidency upon Nixon's resignation. His death in 1979 is widely suspected to have occurred during an act of passion with a woman who was not his wife.

Mayor Wagner: Robert F. Wagner, Jr., was mayor of New York City from 1965 through 1969, and followed that with a career as an ambassador. He died in 1991.

Jackie Kennedy: JFK's wife Jacqueline became a fashion icon during her time as First Lady. Five years following becoming widowed, she married shipping tycoon Aristotle Onassis, who left her a widow again in 1975. She became a book editor, a job she held until she passed away in 1994.

Justice Black: Former U.S. Senator Hugo Black served on the U.S. Supreme Court from 1937 until a week before his death in 1971. He is noted for the decisions he wrote on the establishment clause, including ones curtailing prayer in public schools.

Jimmy Hoffa: Jimmy Hoffa served as General President of the Teamsters Union from 1958 until 1971. For the final four years of his term, he served from prison; his resignation form the post was part of a bargain made with then-president Richard Nixon for his release. Hoffa has not been seen since 1975, and he is presumed to have been murdered.

Estes Kefauver: Failed Democratic vice presidential candidate Kefauver served in the House of Representatives from 1939 to 1949 and in the Senate from 1949 to his death in 1963. Kefauver was the member of the Senate Subcommittee on Juvenile Delinquency who interrogated EC Comics publisher William Gaines during a 1954 hearing on comic books. Gaines's disasterous defense of his horror comics paved the way for self-censorship in the comic book industry, causing the end of most EC titles… but not their humor comic *Mad* which since 1956 has employed Mort Drucker, artist of this book .

Wayne Morse: Morse was elected a US Senator from Oregon in 1944 running as a Republican, switched to being an Independent in 1952, was a Democrat by the time of his second reelection in 1956, and continued serving as a Democrat until losing reelection in 1968. During both his Republican and Democratic days, he frequently found himself at odds with the party leadership. He died in 1974 while in a campaign to regain his Senate seat.

George Romney: The president of American Motors Corporation (whose brands included the rough-and-ready Rambler, but not the high-class Lincoln) from 1945 to 1962 served as Michigan's Governor from 1963 to 1969, when he became US Secretary of Housing and Urban Development. He passed away in 1995, but remained in the news in this century as his son, Mitt, became the Republican nominee for President in 2012.

Orval Faubus: The Democratic Governor of Arkansas from 1955 to 1967 is most commonly recalled for ordering the Arkansas National Guard to keep black students out of Little Rock Central High School in 1957, after the US Supreme Court had ordered the desegregation of America's public schools. Rather than accept the federal government control, Faubus had all of the Little Rock high schools shut down for the 1958-1959 school year. After not running for reelection in 1966, Faubus made three more attempts to regain the govenorship before his death in 1994.

Dean Rusk: Dean Rusk achieved his position of Secretary of State during the Kennedy and Johnson administrations by being the political equivalent of a "safety school", an uncontroversial if uninspiring figure to put forth once Kennedy's first choice, J. William Fulbright, proved too controversial. Rusk died in 1994.

Arthur Schlesinger: A schoolmate of JFK's, Arthur M. Schlesinger served his campaign as speechwriter and propagandist. After the election, he was given the position of Special Assistant, sort of a utility infielder free to handle whatever needed handling. His book on the Kennedy presidency, *A Thousand Days,* is the key insider chronicling of the administration. Schlesinger died in 2007.

Newton Minow: Minow grabbed a lot of press as JFK's Chairman of the Federal Communications Commission; today he is best remembered for calling TV a "vast wasteland." He works in Chicago as an Honorary Consul General of the Republic of Singapore.

Westbrook Pegler: This newspaper columnist criticized every president from Herbert Hoover onward, including JFK. In 1954, he and his syndicate lost a libel suit, paying damages of $175.000 (about $1.5 million today). He lost his column in 1962 after turning his critical attention on executives at his syndicate's parent company, and passed away in 1969.

Martin Luther King: The Reverend Dr. King, whose protesting for civil rights landed him in jail twenty-nine times, was assassinated in 1968. Martin Luther King, Jr. Day has been an annual, federally-recognized holiday since 1986.

Walter Reuther: This United Auto Workers leader was very effective in negotiating strong contracts for the union membership by use of strikes. He died in a fiery Lear-Jet crash in 1970.

Earl Warren: The Chief Justice of the Supreme Court from 1953 until 1969, Warren chaired the government investigation into the assassination of JFK, hence its name, the Warren Commission. He died in 1974.

Walter Winchell: This notorious gossip columnist used his column to go after those he disliked, either for personal or political reasons. His targeting of JFK was at the tail end of his career; his home paper closed down in 1963. (It was in that last year that his column mentioned *The publicity Jackie Kannon got publishing "The JFK Coloring Book" raised his nightspot wage to $3,000 weekly.*) He died in 1974.

Nasser: Gamal Abdel Nasser was president of Egypt from 1956 until his death in 1970.

Jawaharlal Nehru: The Prime Minister of India from 1947 until his death in 1964, Nehru's arrangements for India's annexation of the state of Goa included allowing Goans to maintain their form of civil law, despite having written an article of their Constitution requiring uniformity of civil law.

Ben Gurion: David Ben-Gurion was the first prime minister of Israel... and the third, holding the office from 1948 into 1963 except for two years in the mid-1950s. The man most credited with the founding of the Jewish state died in 1973.

Princess Grace: Beautiful American movie star Grace Kelly married the Prince Rainier III of Monaco in 1956. She died in 1984 following a stroke-induced automobile accident.

Fidel Castro: The revolutionary who brought Communism to Cuba by overthrowing President Fulgencio Batista, Castro served as the island nation's leader (first as "Prime Minister", then as "President") from 1959 until 2008. Castro's willingness to harbor Soviet nuclear arms brought about the Cuban Missile Crisis, the biggest test of JFK's presidential career. He passed the presidency on to his kid brother Raúl years before dying in 2016.

Mao Tse Tung: Chairman Mao served as head of the Communist Party in China – and hence led the nation – from the state's political conversion in 1949 until his death in 1976.

Sukarno: As the president of Indonesia starting with the country's independence in 1945, Sukarno accepted large amount of foreign aid from both the Soviets and the US. Sukarno died in 1970, after having received poor medical care while under health arrest since his ouster from the presidency in 1967.

Farouk: King Farouk I of Egypt had a three month honeymoon with Queen Narriman in 1951, winding up in Cannes. His reign ended the following year, when revolutionaries forced him to abdicate his throne to his six month old son. His death in exile in 1965 is suspected by some to have been a poisoning by Egyptian Intelligence.

Moise Tshombe: As the president of the province of Katanga, Tshombe sought independence from the Congo. His Katangan military was defeated by United Nations forces and he was sent into exile in 1963. He was brought back in as Prime Minister of a Congolese coalition government in 1964, released from that position in 1965, charged with treason later that year, fled the nation, got hijacked to Algeria in 1967, placed under house arrest there, and died while still under house arrest two years later.

Krishna Menon: As Indian Prime Minister Nehru's right-hand man, V. K. Krishna Menon was a fierce and often reviled player on the international scene. Menon died in 1974, at age 78.

Generalissimo Franco: Francisco Franco was Spain's dictator from when he and others overthrew the government in 1939 until he died in 1975.

Shah of Iran: Mohammad Reza Pahlavi was installed as the Iran's supreme leader in 1941 when Soviet and British invading forces caused his father to abdicate. He was overthrown in 1979 and died in exile in Egypt the next year.

Harold Macmillan: The Prime Minister of the United Kingdom from 1957 to 1963, Macmillan dumped seven of his 21 cabinet ministers in July of 1962, in an event that came to be known as "The Night of the Long Knives". He died in 1986.

Charles de Gaulle: De Gaulle served as president of Free France during World War II, then as president of the reunited France from 1959 through 1969. He died the following year.

Chiang Kai-shek: This Generalissimo served as leader of the Republic of China from 1928 until his death in 1975. He lost control of mainland China in 1949; after that, the Republic of China was basically the island of Taiwan, plus a few much smaller islands.

Konrad Adenauer: Chancellor Adenauer led West Germany (the half of the post-war divided Germany which was not in Soviet control) from 1949 until 1963, he oversaw the rebuilding of the war-crippled nation into an economic force to be reckoned with. He died in 1967.

Krushchev: Nikita Krushchev was the Soviet Premier from 1953 until 1964, during the tense Soviet/US political struggle known as the Cold War. After being forced out of office, his name was struck from Soviet history books; when he died in 1971, he was denied a state funeral.